☞ **W9-DIJ-124**

William Penn

Founder of Democracy

Colonial Leaders

Lord Baltimore *English Politician and Colonist*

Benjamin Banneker *American Mathematician and Astronomer*

William Bradford *Governor of Plymouth Colony*

Benjamin Franklin *American Statesman, Scientist, and Writer*

Anne Hutchinson *Religious Leader*

Cotton Mather *Author, Clergyman, and Scholar*

William Penn *Founder of Democracy*

John Smith *English Explorer and Colonist*

Miles Standish *Plymouth Colony Leader*

Peter Stuyvesant *Dutch Military Leader*

Revolutionary War Leaders

Benedict Arnold *Traitor to the Cause*

Nathan Hale *Revolutionary Hero*

Alexander Hamilton *First U.S. Secretary of the Treasury*

Patrick Henry *American Statesman and Speaker*

Thomas Jefferson *Author of the Declaration of Independence*

John Paul Jones *Father of the U.S. Navy*

Thomas Paine *Political Writer*

Paul Revere *American Patriot*

Betsy Ross *American Patriot*

George Washington *First U.S. President*

Colonial Leaders

William Penn

Founder of Democracy

Norma Jean Lutz

Arthur M. Schlesinger, jr.
Senior Consulting Editor

Chelsea House Publishers

Philadelphia

Produced by Robert Gerson Publisher's Services, Avondale, PA

CHELSEA HOUSE PUBLISHERS
Editor in Chief Stephen Reginald
Production Manager Pamela Loos
Director of Photography Judy L. Hasday
Art Director Sara Davis
Managing Editor James D. Gallagher

Staff for *WILLIAM PENN*
Project Editor Anne Hill
Project Editor/Publishing Coordinator Jim McAvoy
Contributing Editor Amy Handy
Associate Art Director Takeshi Takahashi
Series Design Keith Trego

The Chelsea House World Wide Web address is http://www.chelseahouse.com

First Printing
1 3 5 7 9 8 6 4 2

Library of Congress Cataloging-in-Publication Data

Lutz, Norma Jean.
William Penn / by Norma Jean Lutz.
    p. cm.— (Colonial leaders)
Includes bibliographical references (p.) and index.
Summary: A biography of the famous Quaker who founded Pennsylvania
and guaranteed religious freedom to all its settlers.
ISBN 0-7910-5344-X (hc);   ISBN 0-7910-5687-2 (pb)
1. Penn, William, 1644–1718 Juvenile literature. 2. Pioneers—Pennsylvania
Biography Juvenile literature. 3. Quakers—Pennsylvania Biography Juvenile
literature. 4. Pennsylvania—History—Colonial period, ca. 1600–1775 Juvenile
literature.
[1. Penn, William, 1644–1718. 2. Pioneers. 3. Quakers.
4. Pennsylvania—History—Colonial period, ca. 1600–1775.]
I. Title. II. Series.
F152.2.L88 1999
974.8'02'092—dc21
[B]   99-25345
                                                          CIP

To Nicholas Eastburn, with love from your great aunt

Publisher's Note: In Colonial and Revolutionary War America, there were no standard rules for spelling, punctuation, capitalization, or grammar. Some of the quotations that appear in the Colonial Leaders and Revolutionary War Leaders series come from original documents and letters written during this time in history. Original quotations reflect writing inconsistencies of the period.

Contents

William Penn's father was a sea captain and later an admiral. He was a loyal supporter of Charles I, the king of England, at a time when such a position was opposed by many people.

The Admiral

ivil wars were brewing in England when William Penn was born on October 14, 1644. The Penn family lived on Tower Hill in London, near the famous prison known as the Tower of London. William's father, for whom he was named, was a sea captain and was away at sea for months at a time.

At the time of William's birth, the captain remained at home long enough to see his son baptized at a church called All Hallows Barking on Tower Hill. When the baptismal service was completed, the captain rode off on his horse to catch his ship, which anchored along the coast awaiting his boarding.

Because of his Royalist beliefs, Admiral Penn
was briefly imprisoned in the imposing Tower
of London.

For years there had been unrest in England.
King Charles I and his Royalist followers fought
against Oliver Cromwell and his **Puritan** followers. The Royalists believed the king should be
the absolute ruler of all the people. The Puritans
believed the people should have a say in the

government through a Parliament elected by the people. Captain William Penn was a Royalist at heart, but he desired to serve England's navy, no matter who was in power.

The next time the captain came home, his baby son was recovering from a severe case of smallpox. Captain Penn decided to move his family out of crowded London and into the country, where there was clean, fresh air. They moved to a large house in the Parish of Wanstead, about 10 miles from London. At Wanstead there were cows, sheep, horses, vegetable gardens, grain fields, and forests. Young William loved the country. All his life, he would prefer wide open spaces.

On his occasional visits home, William's father told of war victories and of his promotion to the rank of admiral. In spite of his powerful victories in wars against the Dutch, Admiral Penn was arrested on suspicion of being a Royalist. He was imprisoned in the Tower of London. Nothing could be proven and he was soon released, but the suspicion followed him.

In 1649 King Charles was captured by the Puritans and beheaded. Cromwell and the Puritans now controlled the country. The Royalists fled to the Netherlands, where they continued to plot to overthrow Oliver Cromwell.

These events, however, were far removed from the Penns' quiet countryside home. When William turned 11 he was sent to school in the village of Chigwell, four miles from Wanstead. The boy walked to and from school each day, six days a week. This meant he rose very early each morning because classes began at six o'clock. School lasted for 10 hours in summer and eight in winter. Only on Thursdays and Saturdays did the children have an hour off to play.

Chigwell was a private school. There were no public schools in England at that time. The red brick school building was two stories high. The classrooms were dark and dingy, with high windows that let in only a small amount of light. The boys sat on hard, backless wooden benches. Classes were taught in Latin and the students

Oliver Cromwell led the movement against King Charles. When Charles was overthrown, Cromwell ruled England for nearly a decade.

were required to give their recitations in Latin.

Because William enjoyed books and studying, he didn't mind this rigorous schedule. Studying came naturally to him, and he was becoming deeply religious as well. While at Chigwell, he had an experience that he described later as a visit from the Lord. He was alone in the classroom and his inner being was filled with a glowing light as the room grew bright. He would think of this special moment many times in later years.

William's well-organized life was about to meet with drastic changes. Word came to the Wanstead farm that Admiral Penn had been imprisoned once again, this time because the tyrant Oliver Cromwell accused him of disobeying orders. The admiral had been ordered to capture the island of Hispaniola in the Caribbean. Because of the strong Spanish garrison there and because of the heat and disease, Penn's men were unable to take the island.

The admiral decided to take the island of

Jamaica instead, which they did easily. In spite of the fact that Jamaica was a better, richer land than Hispaniola, Cromwell was furious. The navy took away the admiral's command and forced him to retire. Once William's father was released from his second stay in the Tower of London—this one for five weeks—he decided to move his family to Ireland. As long as Cromwell was in power, the admiral knew he would never be safe in England.

Young William had always admired his father and he was deeply affected by this turn of events. In the past, the admiral had come home with news of victories; this time there was defeat and humiliation.

William now had a younger sister and brother. On August 12, 1656, the discouraged admiral loaded his small family on a ship to cross St. George's Channel to Ireland. William's mother, Margaret, was born in Ireland, and she knew the country well. She had often told her son stories of her homeland. Now William would see the green hills of Ireland for himself.

After Charles II took the throne in 1661, a new law was passed forcing everyone to be part of the Church of England, and the Puritans and others were persecuted even more than before. Here, a Quaker named Mary Dyer is being led to prison.

2

Religious Differences

During a time when Admiral Penn was still in favor with Oliver Cromwell, the Puritan leader had given Penn lands in Ireland as a reward for service to England. It was to this place that the family retired in exile. Landing at the cove of Cork, the family traveled up the valley of the River Lee to Macroom, a tiny village of cottages with thatched roofs. In the midst of the village stood a three-story gray stone castle. This became the new home of the Penn family.

Now that the seafaring admiral was land-locked, he had more time for his son. The two spent hours together, during which time William learned to hunt

In 1657 the Penn family moved to Macroom Castle in Ireland. More than 300 years later the village looks much the same.

and to wield a sword. Once again, William Penn fell in love with country life. His studies continued with the assistance of a tutor.

When William was 13, a visitor was invited to Macroom Castle, a **Quaker** by the name of Thomas Loe. It's not clear if this man was invited because the admiral was open-minded or simply because he was bored and had nothing more exciting to do. At any rate, a crowd gathered at Macroom Castle to listen to the man speak. Loe spoke of a true presence of God that each person could experience. He referred to this presence as the "Inner Light." He explained that any person could meet with God anytime and did not need a preacher or a church building.

No doubt at that point, William recalled the moment in the school room when he had felt just such an inner light. Loe went on to say that those who lived by the Inner Light preferred to dress in plain simple clothing and had no need to fight wars and battles. They lived at peace with all men. It would not be the last time William would hear of Thomas Loe.

Although the Penn family lived many miles from England, news reached them of the developments there. The Puritans were experiencing divisions and wars among themselves, with different **factions** splitting off from one another. Some of these factions were very **militant**, such as the one led by Oliver Cromwell. Others were peaceful, such as the Quakers, who were also known as "Friends." Between the two extremes were groups such as the Presbyterians, Baptists, Independents, and Congregationalists.

Samuel Pepys, born in 1633, was an administrator in the Royal Court, a builder of the Royal Navy, and a founding member of the Royal Society. His diaries, written in shorthand, give detailed accounts of important historical events such as the beheading of Charles I, the coronation of Charles II, the plague, and the Great Fire of London. The Penn family is mentioned often in these diaries.

One day the important news came that Oliver Cromwell was dead. Without his strong leadership, the entire political structure collapsed. A letter arrived at Macroom Castle saying that a new parliament had been chosen, and Admiral Penn was to be one of the members. Now William could attend the fine university that his father had always promised.

When the family returned to Tower Hill in London, the admiral threw himself into the political affairs of state. Charles II was to be brought back from France, where he had been in exile since his father's execution. Admiral Penn was commander of the English fleet of 31 ships that sailed out to bring the king home. When the king boarded the admiral's ship, he touched the admiral with his sword and pronounced him a knight. From then on, Admiral Penn would be known as Sir William.

The return of King Charles II was a glorious occasion. Happy crowds thronged the towns, and soldiers on horseback brandished their swords. Flowers were strewn about the streets and bells pealed throughout the city.

The coronation of Charles in April 1661 was even more splendid. William was now a first-year student at Oxford University. He had returned to London for the coronation festivities. Samuel Pepys (pronounced "Peeps"), a neighbor of the Penn family, kept a detailed diary in which he described the important occasion. Pepys, Sir William, son William, and several others had an upper-story room from which to watch the procession. Pepys wrote in his diary, "So glorious was the show with gold and silver, that we were not able to look at it, our eyes at last being so much overcome with it. Both the king and the duke of York took notice of us, as he saw us at the window." The duke of York was James, Charles II's brother, who would become an important person in William Penn's life in the future.

Because he was the son of a high-ranking political person, William was not really expected to study while at school. After all, he was one of the privileged class. And now that the strict Puritans were no longer in power, the people of England enjoyed parties, drinking, frivolity, and the theater. The serious-minded William, however, was not interested in the wild parties of his fellow students. He preferred to lose himself in his studies.

In the months following the coronation of King Charles II, persecution of the Puritans grew more cruel. A new law stated that everyone must worship in the Church of England or

The town of Oxford appeared much like this
when William Penn attended the university there
in the early 1660s.

be severely punished. Even in the small town of Oxford, William saw Puritans being pelted with rocks and Quakers being dragged off to prison. He didn't like what he saw. William firmly believed that people should be able to worship as they chose.

William began attending lectures by a former Oxford professor by the name of John Owen. Owen spoke like Thomas Loe, saying that each man must make his own decisions according to his conscience. From this Puritan teacher, William learned how to boldly express his opinions. Other Oxford students who were Puritans also attended these meetings. William joined with them in refusing to wear the required **surplices** and refusing to attend the required chapel services.

William's rebellious behavior angered his father, who expected his son to conform and to pursue a life of service to the Crown. It is not known for sure whether William was expelled from Oxford or left in disgust. Either way, his father decided to send the boy on a gentleman's tour of Europe. If the younger William was to be a **courtier**, he had to know more about foreign affairs.

In France, William met King Louis XIV. In the king's court William saw ladies and gentlemen dressed in satin, velvet, and lace. At the dinner parties, meat was served in dainty slices rather than in large joints as they were in England. Fine manners were extremely important in France, and William did his best to learn each point.

Upon his return home, William chanced to spend an hour or so visiting with his neighbor, Mr. Pepys. In his diary, Mr. Pepys wrote, "I perceive something of learning he hathe got, but a great deale, if not too much, of the vanity of the French garbe. . . . I fear all real profit he had made of his travel will signify little."

Mr. Pepys was wrong on one point. The travels in Europe did signify a great deal in William's life for they had led him to Saumur, a Protestant

Towering above the river Loire in this modern photo is the château at Saumur, France, now the town museum. In Penn's time it was a Protestant seminary, where he studied under the important religious teacher Moses Amyraut.

seminary in central France. At Saumur he met the headmaster of the academy, Moses Amyraut, the greatest religious teacher of the time. Amyraut taught that the light of God shone in every man's heart to guide him; that a man had to obey his conscience, and his conscience must be guided by God's spirit. Amyraut also believed that a man should always be ready to help his fellow man. These teachings sounded much like those of the Quakers.

Penn spent a year at Saumur studying, reading the Bible, praying, and meditating. While he did not yet adhere to any one religious group, it was certain he was moving away from the Church of England.

William Penn was imprisoned several times because of his religious and political beliefs. From prison he wrote tracts defending what he believed in.

William and the Society of Friends

The next step in William's education would be law school. Sir William arranged for his son to enroll at a prestigious law school called the Inns of Court. William enrolled at Lincoln's Inn in February 1665. William had always been skillful at talking, and he put the talent to good use at law school.

Before the first term was completed, he was called home by his father, who was going into combat against the Dutch—just as he had in the glorious days past. To William's surprise, his father announced that William was to come along. Aboard the *Royal Charles,* William saw firsthand how the men loved and trusted Sir William. After a few weeks at sea, Sir William called his son to his quarters. William learned he was being sent home to deliver a message to the king personally. So this was his father's plan–this was how William would be received in the court of the king. Sir William never stopped planning for his son to be a royal courtier.

William had been back at law school only a few weeks in the spring of 1665 when an epidemic of the **bubonic plague** broke out in the city. Lincoln's Inn closed its doors, as did many schools and businesses. During this time, when hundreds of people were dying and the streets were filled with the dead, the persecution against the Puritans and Quakers never let up. William watched in amazement as Quakers went about nursing the sick in spite of the danger of being arrested. They took food to the houses that were **quarantined**.

By autumn the plague that killed thousands of people had passed and Sir William had arrived home from the Dutch war. The grand naval officer was growing old. His foot was swollen with **gout** and he had to keep it propped up. The father and son discussed the affairs of the family and they decided that William should leave school, travel to Ireland, and take care of property matters there.

King Charles II had given Sir William 7,000 acres of land, which included Shanagarry Castle near the city of Cork. William moved into the castle and set to work. He talked to the farmers who rented the lands, settled disputes between the tenants, issued new leases, and collected rents.

On a visit to Dublin, he fell in with a group of soldiers and helped put down a rebellion of English soldiers. William was so thrilled with the military victory and his part in it, he quickly decided he would become a soldier. He went so far as to have his portrait painted dressed in a full suit of armor. However, another event would change any thoughts he had of joining the military.

This portrait of Penn in armor is a reminder that before he attended his first Quaker meeting, he had decided to become a soldier.

Back in Cork, he learned that Thomas Loe was still holding meetings. William stayed over in the town, determined to attend a meeting. At this meeting, for the first time ever, William felt self-conscious because of his lace-ruffled cuffs, plumed hat, elegant wig, and shining sword. Here the men and women were dressed in plain clothes with no glittering jewels or fancy ruffles.

The meeting began with silence. Just silence. Finally one person rose to speak. Silence followed and then another spoke. Finally Thomas Loe spoke and William Penn was overcome with emotion. Later he described the moment in writing: "The Lord visited me with a certain sound and testimony of his Eternal Word." That was the moment when the 22-year-old Penn decided to join the Society of Friends—an extremely dangerous decision at this time in history. Quakers were persecuted in Ireland just as fiercely as in England.

After he joined, William attended as many of the Quaker meetings as he possibly could. On

September 3, 1667, soldiers broke into a meeting and arrested those in attendance, William Penn included. At the door of Cork prison, Penn took off his sword and handed it to a bystander. He would need it no more.

In prison he wrote a letter to the Lord President of the County of Cork. Because the name of Penn carried so much weight in Ireland, the Quakers were quickly released. But dealing with his father would not be so easy.

In October he received a letter from his father asking him to come home at once. When he returned to London, he saw the ravages of the great London fire which had burned for four days and nights in September 1666. Nearly four-fifths of the city had been destroyed. The Penn home, thankfully, had been spared.

A fellow Quaker traveled home with William and his presence helped to soften the blow of anger and disappointment from Sir William. But later, when they were alone, William's father lashed out with all his seafaring anger. The boy

Although they were fiercely persecuted, the Quakers would not give up their deeply held beliefs, and they continued to hold meetings.

had been trained from childhood to serve as a courtier in the royal court. How could he even think of becoming a Quaker?

But Sir William's angry words did no good. William's mind was made up. Eventually his father ordered him to leave the home. But that posed no problem for William. He simply stayed in the homes of Quaker Friends in London.

Full of **zeal**, he threw himself into the work of the Society. He appeared in public debates and wrote tracts and pamphlets. When he wrote *The Sandy Foundation Shaken,* which refuted many beliefs of the Church of England, it drew a storm of protest. In a matter of days he was arrested and put into the Tower of London. The tiny prison room was cold and miserable. A messenger was sent from the Bishop of London telling Penn he could be released if he would **recant**. Penn answered, "My prison shall be my grave before I will budge a jot." Instead of changing his thinking, his lonely stay in prison only hardened his resolve.

Even though Sir William still did not understand his son's beliefs, he paid a visit to the attic room cell in the Tower of London, which by summer had turned into an oven. Sir William sent a petition to the king's Privy Council requesting his son's release, but no release came.

Finally, Penn wrote another tract clearing up the misconceptions of his first and sent it off to Whitehall. Upon reading the new tract the king met with his council, and on July 28, 1669, they decided William Penn could go free.

After his release Penn planned to return to Ireland and visit friends there, but first he made a side trip to the village of Amersham in Buckingham County. He stopped at the home of a Quaker family by the name of Pennington. Gulielma Springett (Mrs. Pennington's daughter by a previous marriage) was an attractive girl just William's age. He'd met her previously at the home of London Friends, and he'd been quite taken with her. This visit gave him a chance to speak with her and the two agreed to write to each other.

In Ireland, Penn visited imprisoned Quakers, then made it his business to free them. He called on the skills he learned at law school and used his connections in high places. Eventually these Quakers were released.

Upon his return to England, in August 1670, he was imprisoned once again. He had gathered with a group of Quakers in front of a meeting house that had been boarded up by the authorities. When Penn joined them, he began preaching and was immediately arrested. This time he was taken to London's Newgate Prison, a foul dungeon where the debtors, murderers, and highwaymen were housed. The trial began the very next day.

William Penn pleaded not guilty to a charge of disturbing the peace. Since he knew the law, he argued his own case. The judge threatened the jury, telling them that if they did not bring back a verdict of guilty they would be imprisoned without food or water. This type of harassment of jury members was often done in the days of Charles II. Penn, however, would not have it. He spoke out boldly, reminding the jurors of the Magna Carta, an ancient charter of the English people guaranteeing certain rights and privileges.

These brave jurors, supported by Penn's courage, returned a verdict of not guilty. When faced with prison, they retained lawyers and appealed the case to a higher court. Eventually an important decision was handed down stating that a jury must be allowed to render a free verdict and not be punished for that verdict. This important trial made history in the English justice system. And it was all due to the courage and determination of William Penn.

In spite of the victory, Penn and another Quaker were still locked up in Newgate Prison. They had been unjustly fined for contempt of court and imprisoned because they could not pay the fine. Thankfully, Penn was released in time to be by his father's side when he died September 16, 1670.

George Fox founded a group originally called "Children of Light." Later this Society of Friends became known as the Quakers. From Fox's meetings, Penn learned about Quakers in the colonies.

A Home for the Quakers

On April 4, 1672, William Penn and Guli Springett were wed in a simple Quaker ceremony. There is no minister at a Quaker wedding. The bride and groom speak their own vows, promising to be loving and faithful as long as they both live. After the vows, and after times of silent meditation, different members stand and speak blessings and encouragement.

The couple made their home in a large house near the village of Rickmansworth. While their lives became more quiet and settled, they were close enough to London to keep in touch with Quakers there. A Quaker named Philip Ford had become

Gulielma Springett married her childhood friend William Penn and they had six children who survived to adulthood.

Penn's aide. With a good helper, Penn was free to spend more time dealing with Quaker matters.

After William and Guli had been married about a year, the great leader of the Society of Friends, George Fox, returned from a visit to America. Penn attended the meetings of George Fox and heard him tell about the increasing number of Quakers living in the New World. These reports were exciting to William Penn. Massachusetts had been given to the Puritans. Maryland had been given to Lord Baltimore as a refuge for the Catholics. Penn thought perhaps there could be a colony for Quakers as well.

A few weeks after Fox's return, Penn learned that the Quaker leader had been arrested. In a meeting of the Friends it was decided that William Penn should make a personal appeal to the king. It had been six long years since he had visited the Royal Court. Penn wasn't sure how he would be received. He chose to meet with the duke of York–James, the king's brother.

The duke received Penn and assured him that he too was against persecution and agreed to help persuade the king to pardon Fox. A pardon did come, but not before Fox had spent 14 months in a dark and dirty dungeon. When Penn saw how Fox's health suffered, he became more determined to have a colony where people could enjoy freedom of speech and worship.

In the Penn home, William and Guli had grieved over the loss of three children who died in infancy. At last a son whom they named Springett, born January 25, 1675, grew to be robust and healthy. In 1678 a daughter, Letitia, was born. A second son, William Jr., came along in the spring of 1680.

During this time, Penn had become involved in a dispute between two Quakers who owned land in the western part of New Jersey. Because Quakers did not take one another to a court of law, Penn became the **impartial arbitrator** between the two. Penn's legal experience and his experience in handling his father's lands in Ireland came in handy. After settling the dispute, he and two other Quaker leaders were asked to govern the colony.

George Fox was born to a Puritan family. At 19, he went in search of a church where he would be happy. He searched throughout England. Then he heard a voice say, "There is one, even Christ Jesus, that can speak to thy condition." He wrote this revelation in his journal—that God dwelled within every person. He preached this message to all who would listen. He became the founder of the Society of Friends.

Together they wrote up a plan of government that guaranteed freedoms that were not allowed in England–freedom of speech, freedom of religion, and impartial justice for every citizen under the law. The plan was called Concessions and Agreements. The document stated, "we put the power in the people." One important point set this government apart from others in the New World: Indians were to be treated fairly. There would be one set of laws for everyone. The document was signed by 151 people.

When 230 New Jersey pioneers set sail aboard the *Kent,* Penn was not among them. Much work remained to be done in England. He and Guli had moved from Rickmansworth to a big brick house in the parish of Worminghurst. The house was high on a hill and commanded a grand view in all directions. Since there was no Quaker meeting house in the area, the Quakers gathered each week in the Worminghurst house.

Letters arrived from the West New Jersey colony telling of the successes there. After buying land rights from the Indians, the settlers built the town of Burlington. Homes and shops were constructed and fruit trees planted. West

To pay off a debt owed to Penn's father, King Charles II granted Penn's request for land in the New World. Penn is seen here receiving the charter of Pennsylvania from the king.

New Jersey seemed like a good place, but it wasn't large enough to hold all the Quakers who wanted to leave England.

Penn knew of land on the western side of the Delaware River. It was land that belonged to the duke of York. Since Penn was a Whig, meaning he supported a government run by Parliament rather than by the king, he was sure the king would never give him a land grant. It was then that Penn remembered the debt of 16,000 pounds that Sir William had loaned to the king years earlier. While his father would never have asked for the money to be returned, William Penn would. That was the only way he could possibly receive the land grant. He wrote a formal petition and sent it to King Charles. To everyone's amazement, the request was granted. The royal charter, dated March 4, 1681, made 36-year-old William Penn owner of a vast tract of land. Here he could begin his "Holy Experiment."

Penn set sail for the colonies in the fall of 1682. This drawing shows him in Pennsylvania, holding the deed to his American land.

The New Colony, Pennsylvania

usy days followed the granting of the charter. William Penn spent hours pouring over maps, charts, and plans. He wrote tracts and sent them out to explain the terms under which land could be obtained. The idea of private property as we know it today was a new idea just beginning to develop. In Penn's new colony, the landholders would pay what was known as quitrent, or fixed rent.

King Charles was insistent that the colony be named "Pennsylvania" for his old friend Sir William. "Sylvania" is from the Latin word for "woods." Penn, who feared that people would think it was named for him, suggested it be named New Wales.

But the king would not be **dissuaded** and the name remained.

The name of the capital city was definitely Penn's choice. Philadelphia is taken from two Greek words, *philos* ("love") and *adelphos* ("brother"): the city of brotherly love. Penn planned for the capital to be set in a high, dry, and healthy location. Remembering the narrow, crooked, smelly streets of London, he designed Philadelphia to be laid out in straight broad streets. Plots would be large enough for trees and gardens to grow within the city. He called it a "green country town." This was the first time a town had ever been laid out in advance. This pattern was later followed in scores of American towns as the country grew westward.

Penn planned for prisons in the colony to provide workshops to teach prisoners a trade. This was an entirely new idea. In the past, prisoners were simply locked up and forgotten. No one had ever thought to present them with a new way of life.

Penn planned the layout of Philadelphia carefully, and even today the city still has some of the wide, tree-lined streets he envisioned.

Nearest to Penn's heart was the government itself. The idea of a government of the people and by the people had been his dream for many years. Penn referred to the colony as a "Holy Experiment" because it truly was an experimental move toward democracy, something that had never been done before. In a letter of 1681 to those who were already living in the colony, he wrote, "You shall be governed by laws of your own making." Penn called it the Frame of Government.

Based on the New Jersey Concessions, the Frame contained a preface and 24 sections. The government was to have a council and general assembly, an upper and lower house. There would be elections every year to select members of the council and assembly. As the governor, Penn would preside over the council. Wisely, he left the Frame open for amendments. In later years, much of the Frame of Government would become the basis of the Constitution of the United States.

Penn appointed his first cousin, William Markham, as deputy governor of the colony. In the summer of 1681, Markham set sail for America. By that fall, two more shiploads of Quakers followed. Soon Penn would be going as well. Meanwhile, letters went back and forth between Penn and Markham as Penn continued to give instructions. Penn was adamant that the Indians be treated kindly and fairly. He even wrote letters to the Indians to reassure them of his desire to live peacefully with them. This attitude was quite the opposite of the Puritans, who looked upon the Indians with disdain.

Finally, in the fall of 1682, Penn had his affairs in order and he was ready to sail to America himself. All his financial affairs were in the hands of his trusted aide, Philip Ford. Guli was expecting another child and could not go. It was Penn's hope that he could send for his family soon.

He boarded the *Welcome* to travel to America, a trip that took two long months. The ship was crowded and uncomfortable. An outbreak of smallpox made things much worse. But since Penn had had the disease as a child, he was immune.

It was late October when Penn landed at New Castle, where William Markham greeted him. From there he sailed up the Delaware River to see the site for the capital city. At that time there were only 10 houses standing, but Penn was very pleased with the location. Philadelphia's size would soon change. This special city would become the seat of government throughout the Revolutionary War, nearly a century later.

From there Penn traveled up the river another 25 miles to see Pennsbury Manor, where the Penn family home would be built. Again, Penn was pleased. He dreamed of Guli and the children joining him there.

His dealings with the Indians began almost immediately. The Indian leaders were anxious to meet him. He found it easy to make himself

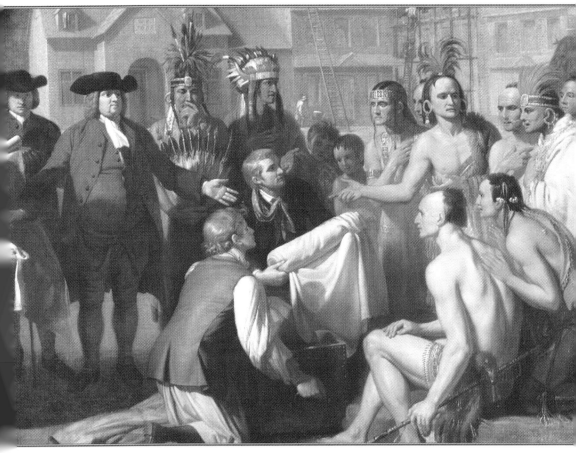

Penn showed the Indians great respect and they thought well of him in return. This painting by Benjamin West depicts a treaty negotiation.

at home among them. He visited their communities and ate their food in their ways. He joined in their sports and impressed them with his athletic abilities. He took time to learn the Lenape language so he could converse with them directly and not through an interpreter.

Between 1682 and 1684, Penn held nine Indian treaties. He purchased the land from them piece by piece, and did so in accordance with Indian custom and etiquette. At no time did he treat the Indians with anything but respect and dignity. They affectionately called him Brother Onas (onas meaning "quill" or "penn").

By the time Penn had been in the Colonies for two full years, the city of Philadelphia had grown to a population of 2,500 people. Outside the city, farmlands and estates were being established. Everything was going well except for one sticky problem—boundaries.

The charter had not been clear about the border between Pennsylvania and Maryland, and Lord Baltimore was protesting. Penn attempted to meet with Lord Baltimore and settle the matter. Lord Baltimore not only disputed the border, but Penn's right to the land along Delaware Bay. This was land that Penn had purchased from the duke of York. The Maryland charter had been given to Lord Baltimore's father in 1632. Therefore he felt the land had belonged to him before it came into the hands of the duke of York.

Even though Penn wanted to stay in America, it became evident that he would have to return to England to settle the matter in the king's Privy Council. Lord Baltimore had already set sail for England.

Penn left instructions to his gardener, Ralph Smyth, to set out the gardens around Pennsbury, and to make graveled walkways and build steps at the water side. He was sure he'd be back in a short time. With heavy heart, he left his new home.

Perched high above the city, a majestic statue of William Penn stands atop City Hall on Broad Street, surveying modern Philadelphia and his "Holy Experiment."

Keeping the Peace

Upon his return to England Penn found the king in poor health. The "merry monarch," as he'd been called, had dissolved Parliament and was ruling as absolute monarch. He'd lost all interest in the American colonies. It was evident that the settlement would take much longer than Penn had first thought. Four months later, King Charles II was dead.

Since there was no son to take the throne, Charles's brother James II came to power. This caused great alarm throughout England because James was Catholic. The people feared that James would make the official church a Catholic one.

In the midst of the turmoil, Penn and Baltimore appeared before the Privy Council and part of the dispute was solved. The council decided to split Delaware between the two colonies. They gave Penn the eastern part along the Delaware River, and gave the western part along the Chesapeake Bay to Baltimore.

Peter the Great was tsar of Russia. In 1697 he visited Europe and England to learn more about other cultures. While in England he attended a meeting of Quakers. William Penn and the tsar met and discussed Quaker beliefs. While Peter the Great appreciated the books Penn gave him, he said he could see no use for a group of people who would not go to war for their country.

James II turned out to be a terrible king. Since James had no male heir to the throne, most people felt it was only a matter of time before he would be displaced and his older daughter, Mary, would come to power. Mary was married to William of Orange in Holland and both were Protestants. However, before that could happen, James II and his second wife had a son, an heir to the throne.

Penn patiently coun-seled with his old friend the king, but James refused to listen. Revolt spread throughout the country, and finally the people invited Mary and William to come with an army and be the rulers of the land. In November 1688, William of Orange landed in England with 14,000 troops. James's officers deserted him and he was forced to flee to France.

George Calvert (1580–1632), Lord Baltimore, founded the colony of Maryland.

William and Mary ruled together as William III and Mary II. They signed a Bill of Rights that guaranteed that no king would ever over-rule the will of the Parliament. This was called the "Glorious Revolution." However, to Penn, it was not so glorious. Since he'd been such close friends with James II, he was now suspected of treason. Would he lose the colony altogether?

Penn remained home at Worminghurst, hoping the danger would pass. But since James was in France planning to recapture his throne, all of his friends were under suspicion. In the next few years, Penn would be arrested three different times. He continued to make plans to gather a group to leave for America, but the plans kept falling through. At last he was forced to go into hiding.

Poverty dogged his heels, and Guli's health was failing. To add to his misery, word came that William and Mary had taken over the government of Pennsylvania and planned to set military rule over it. For three years Penn remained in seclusion until finally his name was cleared from all suspicion of plotting to overthrow the king and queen. William and Mary even agreed to issue a new charter for the colony. However, six months before the charter was issued, Penn's beloved Guli died, on February 23, 1694. Penn

Reconstructed in the 1930s, the Penn home stands on the grounds of his estate, Pennsbury Manor, in Morrisville, Pennsylvania.

was grieved that she never saw the beautiful home he'd built for them at Pennsbury Manor.

Through the years, Philip Ford continued to serve as an aide and accountant for Penn. On various occasions, Ford asked Penn to sign documents without explaining fully what they

Two years after he was widowed, Penn married Hannah Callowhill in a Friends ceremony. An artist imagined the scene looked like this.

contained. Penn trusted Ford. Now Ford was claiming that Penn owed him more than 10,000 pounds—an enormous sum of money.

On September 3, 1699, Penn was ready to

board the *Canterbury* and sail to America. With him was his new wife, Hannah, and daughter, Letitia. His beloved son Springett had died three years earlier. His younger son, William Penn, Jr., was married and expecting a child. To Penn's disappointment, his namesake had turned out to be an unruly, disrespectful, and irresponsible son.

When Penn arrived back in Philadelphia, his joy was complete. By now it was an important city in the New World, second in size only to Boston. To Penn's relief there was still no militia, and no stockades. And the Indians remained friendly. The January after their arrival, Hannah gave birth to a son, John, the only one of Penn's children born in the New World. By summer, they had moved into Pennsbury Manor.

Penn was kept busy as the head administrator in the colony. He worked to keep peace between the Quakers and the non-Quakers. Governors of other colonies came to visit, and Indian tribes met at the manor for their conferences.

Penn had always believed that uniting the colonies was the best way to deal with the common problems they shared. In a meeting with the governors of Massachusetts, New York, and Virginia, they drew up just such a plan. However, when the plan reached the king's Privy Council, the council was thinking of nothing but an **impending** war with France.

This was terrible news. War between England and France meant war between the English and French in America as well. That meant Pennsylvania would be expected to fight in that war. If they refused to offer military aid, the colony might be taken away again. Penn would have to return to England to defend himself. He and Hannah, Letitia, and baby John sailed aboard the *Dolmahoy* in November 1701. Penn never again saw his beloved colony.

Lack of money plagued Penn from the moment he returned. He had hoped the quitrents would help to support him. However, it was just the opposite—he had poured a great deal of his own money into the colony with very little to show for it. James Logan, a Scottish Quaker and trusted friend of Penn's, was left in charge of the colony. Logan attempted to send goods to Penn, such as furs, tobacco, and flour. But English ships were being seized by the French, so none got through. Penn was so poor that Hannah had to live with her family in Bristol.

Philip Ford had died but his family made cruel threats against Penn for the money they claimed he owed them. Penn called on the assistance of other learned Quakers, who thoroughly searched past records and accounts. They were shocked to discover that for years Philip Ford had stolen money from Penn by using illegal bookkeeping methods.

While the Quakers did their best to bring about a settlement, it seemed inevitable that it would have to be taken to a court of law. Penn was confident he would win. Queen Anne had come to power, the younger daughter of Penn's friend James II. Penn was once again in favor at the Royal Court.

The case dragged on for more than three years. Penn's lawyers were worried because he had signed so many papers without examining them. Could he convince the court to side with him? Penn was now the father of four children by Hannah. In January 1706 their fifth child, Richard, was born. Hannah moved back to London and the family lived in a house in Ealing, just outside London. A sixth child, Dennis, was born there a year later.

In 1705 Penn sent young William to Pennsylvania, hoping his son could take over some of the administrative duties there. Instead the young man fell into bad company and caused a turmoil. None of Penn's friends could trust William Jr. James Logan wrote letters to Penn relaying bad news about the boy. Finally Penn called his son home.

On January 7, 1708, Penn was arrested while sitting in a Quaker meetinghouse and taken to debtors' prison. He was now 63 years old. The Ford family took this opportunity to come before Queen Anne and ask for a new charter for the colony of Pennsylvania. Queen Anne ignored them, and the family received a severe rebuff from the court. This may have frightened them, for eventually they arbitrated by accepting 6,700 pounds as a settlement. Nine Quakers helped to pay this sum, to whom Penn gave new mortgages on his Pennsylvania property.

At last his troubles seemed to be over. Now Penn found a home for his family, a large house in the wooded countryside in Ruscombe halfway between London and Oxford. From here he corresponded often with Logan and kept busy with the business of the Society of Friends.

On a visit to Hannah's parents in Bristol, as Penn was writing a letter to James Logan, the quill slipped from his hand and he fell forward on the desk. He had suffered a stroke. By January

Each year many children visit the Liberty Bell, which was installed in 1751 to commemorate Penn's famous charter.

Hannah was able to take him home to Ruscombe, hoping he would **recuperate**. Yet another stroke caused him to lose his memory and he became **incompetent**. Although he continued to lose strength and his memory slipped away, Hannah lovingly cared for him. On July 30, 1718, William Penn died. He was buried at Jordans, Buckinghamshire, in a Quaker cemetery.

Penn's descendants continued to hold official ownership of the colony of Pennsylvania until the Revolutionary War, when all royal charters were absolved. In 1751, to celebrate the 50th anniversary of Penn's *Charter of Privileges,* a bell was hung in the State House at Philadelphia. On the bell these words were engraved: "Proclaim liberty throughout the land unto all the inhabitants thereof." This Liberty Bell, as we call it today, makes us think of 1776 and Independence Day. It should, instead, make us think back to the true pioneer of an independent form of government, William Penn.

GLOSSARY

arbitrator a person chosen to settle a debate

bubonic plague a very contagious disease, usually fatal, caused by bacteria carried by fleas and infected rodents

courtier an attendant in the court of a king or other sovereign

dissuade to discourage a person from a course of action

faction a smaller troublesome group within a larger group

gout a painful disease that makes the foot swell

impartial not favoring either side

impending something that is about to take place

incompetent not fit; not capable

militant warlike; ready to fight

Puritan a member of a group of English Protestants in the sixteenth and seventeenth centuries who wished to simplify ceremonies and other aspects of the Church of England

Quaker a member of the Society of Friends

quarantine a period of time during which persons or objects are isolated so as not to spread a contagious disease

recant to make a formal denial of a previously held belief

recuperate to return to health; to recover

surplices a loose-fitting white gown with wide sleeves worn by some clergymen

zeal enthusiasm for, and devotion to, a cause

CHRONOLOGY

1644 William Penn is born in a house on Tower Hill in London, England.

1649 Charles I is beheaded.

1656 Penn family goes into exile in Ireland.

1658 Oliver Cromwell dies.

1660 Penn attends Oxford.

1661 Charles II is crowned king of England.

1662 Penn is sent to France by his father.

1665 Penn studies law at Lincoln's Inn; Great Plague of London kills thousands of citizens.

1666 The Great Fire of London destroys most of the city.

1667 Penn is arrested in Ireland; he declares he is a Quaker.

1672 Penn marries Gulielma Springett.

1681 Royal Charter for Pennsylvania is presented to Penn.

1682 Penn travels to America.

1684 Penn returns to England to settle boundary dispute.

1694 Gulielma dies.

CHRONOLOGY

1699 Along with his second wife, Hannah, and daughter Letitia, Penn returns to America.

1701 Penn returns to England.

1718 Penn dies at his home in Ruscombe, England.

COLONIAL TIME LINE

1607 Jamestown, Virginia, is settled by the English.

1620 Pilgrims on the *Mayflower* land at Plymouth, Massachusetts.

1623 The Dutch settle New Netherland, the colony that later becomes New York.

1630 Massachusetts Bay Colony is started.

1634 Maryland is settled as a Roman Catholic colony. Later Maryland becomes a safe place for people with different religious beliefs.

1636 Roger Williams is thrown out of the Massachusetts Bay Colony. He settles Rhode Island, the first colony to give people freedom of religion.

1682 William Penn forms the colony of Pennsylvania.

1688 Pennsylvania Quakers make the first formal protest against slavery.

1692 Trials for witchcraft are held in Salem, Massachusetts.

1712 Slaves revolt in New York. Twenty-one blacks are killed as punishment.

COLONIAL TIME LINE

1720 Major smallpox outbreak occurs in Boston. Cotton Mather and some doctors try a new treatment. Many people think the new treatment shouldn't be used.

1754 French and Indian War begins. It ends nine years later.

1761 Benjamin Banneker builds a wooden clock that keeps precise time.

1765 Britain passes the Stamp Act. Violent protests break out in the colonies. The Stamp Act is ended the next year.

1775 The battles of Lexington and Concord begin the American Revolution.

1776 Declaration of Independence is signed.

FURTHER READING

Bruchac, Joseph. *The Arrow Over the Door*. New York: Dial Books for Young Readers, 1998.

Clay, Rebecca. *Kidding Around Philadelphia: A Young Person's Guide to the City*. Santa Fe: John Muir Publishing; New York: Norton, 1990.

Day, James. *The Black Death*. New York: Bookwright Press, 1989.

James, Ian. *Inside Great Britain*. New York: Franklin Watts, 1988.

Weiss, David A. *The Great Fire of London*. New York: Cumberland Enterprises, 1992.

Williams, Jean Kinney. *The Quakers*. New York: Franklin Watts, 1998.

INDEX

INDEX

PICTURE CREDITS

ABOUT THE AUTHOR

NORMA JEAN LUTZ, who lives in Tulsa, Oklahoma, has been writing professionally since 1977. She is the author of more than 250 short stories and articles as well as over 30 books–fiction and nonfiction. Of all the writing she does, she most enjoys writing children's books.

Senior Consulting Editor **ARTHUR M. SCHLESINGER, JR.** is the leading American historian of our time. He won the Pulitzer Prize for his book *The Age of Jackson* (1945) and again for *A Thousand Days* (1965). This chronicle of the Kennedy Administration also won a National Book Award. He has written many other books including a multi-volume series, *The Age of Roosevelt.* Professor Schlesinger is the Albert Schweitzer Professor of the Humanities at the City University of New York, and has been involved in several other Chelsea House projects, including the REVOLUTIONARY WAR LEADERS biographies on the most prominent figures of early American history.